I. B Price

Some Recollections of a blameless Life

I. B Price

Some Recollections of a blameless Life

ISBN/EAN: 9783337054670

Printed in Europe, USA, Canada, Australia, Japan

Cover: Foto ©ninafisch / pixelio.de

More available books at **www.hansebooks.com**

SOME RECOLLECTIONS OF A BLAMELESS LIFE

———

EDITED BY

I. B. PRICE

PROFESSOR OF MATHEMATICS IN UNION COLLEGE

———

" Yes; Thou art still the Life, Thou art the Way
The holiest know; Light, Life, the Way of heaven!
And they who dearest hope and deepest pray
Toil by the Light, Life, Way, which Thou hast given "

———

UNION COLLEGE, SCHENECTADY, N. Y.
1884

PREFACE.

WHEN I yielded to the earnest solicitations of some friends to edit this brief Memoir of one for whom I had the greatest respect and love, I hoped that my health would permit me to give it the care and attention it so richly deserves; but I have not been granted the needed strength. Friends have done much of the work, and if we have together presented in such clear light the many rare and noble qualities of our dead friend that young men may see and seek to imitate them, our object will be fully realized.

UNION COLLEGE,
    July 15th, 1884.

INTRODUCTION.

*g*N the autumn of 1872 Mr. Joseph R. Davis, a youth thoroughly vigorous in physique, and rendered attractive by his strong, though not handsome face, entered Union College. His examinations for admission, passed in the previous June, had impressed the examiners with the thorough character of his preparation. His sun-browned face marked him as fresh from the farm, and suggested to his future instructors that he was, perhaps, another of that multitude who leave the green fields to join their more active fellow men in solving life problems of a higher nature than those which relate to seed-time and harvest. The most valuable prizes given by the College at that time were those known as the " Nott Prize Scholarships," and having a total money value of four hundred and twenty dollars. The student in order to secure one of them must possess fine ability and almost a faultless preparation in the Classics and the Mathematics usually required in preparation for college. At an examination held early in January, 1873. Mr. Davis was awarded one of those prizes.

Indeed, from the hour he entered the College, Mr. Davis was marked as one about whom many hopes centered. No one knew then that it was the decree of the Master, in Whose will he delighted, that when he had fully prepared himself for the work of this life he should be called to the life above. His boyhood was full of obedience to parents ; his youth and young manhood were spent in acquiring a brilliant preparation for after success in his college life. After graduation he taught one year in Franklin, Delaware county, and then he was called to the tutorship of Latin in his *alma mater.* At the end of the third year as tutor he entered Union Theological Seminary, and after graduation, under the advice of his physician, he spent a few months at Riverside, in Southern California, and then in great feebleness he journeyed wearily and alone back to the quiet rest and love of his home among the hills of Western Pennsylvania. There scarcely seems enough in this brief outline to distinguish him from many others ; yet he was such a rare scholar ; there was such sweet purity about his acts and thoughts ; such noble consecration of every faculty to each undertaking, that from his many friends there comes a resistless plea for some clear outline of his scholarship and Christian character—some brief narration of the marked influence he silently exerted for Christ's cause, and of the work he did that His kingdom might soon come among men.

The materials for this Memoir have been gathered from those who knew Mr. Davis intimately, and they were kind enough to place them in the form in which I have used them.

Professor Whitehorne, of the Greek Department in Union College, and one full of love for the memory of his brilliant student, has written of his college work ; Rev. Dr. T. G. Darling, of the First Presbyterian Church of this city, gives a full and helpful account of the work Mr. Davis did in that church during his college course and while he was still in the seminary; Rev. Dr. George Alexander, formerly a valued professor in Union College, the Rev. Dr. Hastings, of Union Theological Seminary, and Rev. Mr. Morris, of Neath, have all given valuable help. Many others have made contributions which appear in the course of the Memoir. The father of Mr. Davis furnished the account of the formation of the Welsh colony at Neath and the short family history which is given.

A MEMOIR.

CHAPTER I.

FAMILY HISTORY.

𝓰N September, 1831, the "Elizabeth Clark," a brig, commanded by Capt. Richardson, sailed from Swansea, on the coast of Wales, with seventy passengers. They were bound for America, and most of them were Welsh. The voyage lasted eight weeks and ended at New York. At that time, of course, railroads only existed in the minds of enthusiasts, and there was needed then the brain and muscle of half a century to yet fully develop them. It was a time when the emigrant found but little to cheer or encourage him as he pushed on to the end of his wearisome journey.

After a brief rest in New York, they took passage on the Hudson, and in a little while they left the River and travelled by canal till their route was frozen. A few families took sleighs and pushed on to Pike township, Bradford county, Pennsylvania. The name of the township has since been changed to Neath. The country was almost entirely unbroken forest—desolate and uninviting.

With those who journeyed on in sleighs was a young minister, Daniel Jones, a man of culture and fine education. Among the families in the new settlement was that of William Evans, the father of the late Professor Evans of Cornell University, and Samuel Davis, the grandfather of the subject of this Memoir. Almost immediately after their arrival they organized a church, in which Mr. Jones preached to them in their native tongue. The building which they erected as a church served the double purpose of a place for worship and a school house. The seats employed were made from " slabs " from the saw-mill. It is probably safe to say that the question of free seats *versus* hired pews never agitated the minds of the worshipers. Mr. William S. Davis, in the letter in which he gave me a brief history of his family, and of the Neath colony of Welsh, made this comment : " Uninviting and even uncomfortable as was our house of worship at that time, would to God that there were the same zeal and enthusiasm in the people of to-day for the worship of the living God as there was at that time when they would go for miles through the woods, amid mud and snow, on foot, on any evening of the week as well as on the Sabbath to wait on the Lord." As we have already stated, Joseph R. Davis was the grandson of Mr. Samuel Davis. The family of the latter consisted of his wife and five children, three of whom 'were boys. With the coming of the spring of 1832, Mr. Davis purchased a farm of ninety-five acres. It was in reality ninety-five acres of wilderness, awaiting the tireless effort of the new owner to become a home, growing as the years went on, rich in all the comforts and culture which belong to a

Christian home. The youngest son of Samuel Davis, William S. Davis, married Elizabeth Philips, who was also among the little band which reached Neath in the early winter of 1831. The subject of the Memoir, Joseph R. Davis, was their first-born, the date of his birth being August 11th, 1853. All of the people about the little child were Welsh, and as a consequence he first learned to talk in the Welsh language. He was so thorough a Welshman that when he commenced going to school his teacher was much troubled to understand the child, or in turn to make himself understood, but at the end of three months he thoroughly understood the English, but to the end of his life the language of his childhood days, with all of its seeming crookedness, was full of interest to him. This was the more remarkable, as most of his life was spent away from home with people who knew nothing of the Welsh language. He always wrote to his parents and pastor in Welsh. His pastor, the Rev. Samuel A. Williams, always spoke in high terms of the good Welsh letters he received from the boy at college.

From childhood he evinced a desire to unite with the church, and at the age of thirteen he was received as a member, and from that time he took an active part in church work, and by his noble example of purity in thought and speech did great good. His father writes : " His first work was in the prayer meetings of the church, and next he assisted me at the family altar, and was, as we believe, not only ready and willing at all times and places to witness for the Master, but it was a delight and pleasure for him to do so."

CHAPTER II.

TOWANDA, PA.,
July 14, 1884. }

My Dear Professor Price:

MY acquaintance and association with Joseph R. Davis began when we were school boys in the Le Raysville Academy, at Le Raysville, Pa., pursuing substantially the same studies, and with them substantially the same object, a preparation for college. Having been tutored by a Union graduate, the Rev. H. F. Cochrane, of the Class of '58, who was always faithful to his *alma mater*, our studies and tastes were naturally shaped and directed in large measure by his preference. We were examined for entrance and matriculated on the same day, and roomed together during our entire course. We graduated friends as we had entered, and though less closely associated after graduation, yet our friendly relations suffered no abridgment to the last.

It is seldom there are seen combined in the same individual with natural capabilities the virtues of industry, temperance, worthy ambition, perseverance, truthfulness and Christian zeal in so eminent a degree as exhibited in the character and brief life of J. R. Davis. With a naturally strong physical

(12)

constitution, though it early succumbed to unremitting strain
and overwork, he was industrious beyond his fellows, whether
in college or in other fields of effort. He had no companion-
ship with idlers, and only sparingly engaged in social
recreation. Often he spent with his books and in the class
room, day after day and week after week, from fourteen to
sixteen hours out of the twenty-four. He was not satisfied
with anything less than a perfect recitation, and this he
seldom failed to accomplish by steady application and regular
work. With great aversion to excess of every kind (unless it
were excess of work), he was always temperate in thought,
speech and habits of life. His thoughts were pure and
charitable ; his speech always chaste and moderate ; his
habits of life correct and exemplary. With natural endow-
ment and fondness for learning, he was ambitious for
knowledge, even to the extent of desiring to excel others.
Scholastic attainment always elicited his admiration. With no
particular striking mental adaptation in one direction, he was
proficient in many. His was not the intellect sometimes seen
that bridges and spans intermediate mathematical processes,
as it were, without mental effort, and writes out the result
with equal accuracy and rapidity, but perchance in Livy or
Herodotus is dull and slow. Neither was his mind of the
order that grasps and remembers the etymology and translation of a Greek or Latin verb, but utterly fails in a
geometrical demonstration or algebraic formula. But with
well-balanced, sufficient capabilities for any branch of learning,
his knowledge and mastery of it were gained by painstaking

study and prolonged research.   He spurned to "ride" through any lesson.   There was no place on his library shelf, or in his trunk, "for a horse."   The light *equestrian* student might catch a glimpse of the flowers in a line from Horace, but only the plodding foot traveller could really enjoy their fragrance or perceive the very subtlety of their meaning. Whatever subject was assigned to the class in his course, he mastered it of his own powers, and was invariably successful in class recitation.   Though not acquiring with the utmost ease he had a receptive mind, and his memory was strong and apt to be correct.

Without ostentatious self-confidence, he relied upon his own resources, and was persistent and persevering in accomplishing whatever he undertook.   Slow to give up a difficult problem or abandon a doubtful passage, he was seldom obliged to, and professors and classmates alike came to count upon Davis' having the correct solution or proper translation.

Of Welsh parentage and surroundings, he spoke the language of his father's people with natural ease, and during all the course of his other studies, while those of his age and generation in the vicinity of his home were to a considerable degree losing the language, he not only kept up his acquaintance with it, but to a fair degree familiarized himself with its etymology and grammatical composition, maintaining during the four years of his college course a correspondence with his father in this tongue.

Not of a jovial turn, his life was for the most part a serious one.   Solitude often seemed congenial to his spirits.   At times he seemed oppressed with a lack of cheerfulness, and I remember on one occasion his comparing a certain phase of his own life with the sadness marking a character of which he had then been lately reading. He made few confidants, and violated the confidence of none. Cherishing ambitions and desires of a high character, only now and then glimpses were revealed of his aims.

His moral qualities ranked not inferior to his mental. He had not the frankness of nature possessed by some — that communicative disposition which reveals everything and keeps back nothing — but he never warped the truth, and his word, when spoken, could be relied upon. He never exhibited all there was of him at the first meeting with a stranger, but left the impression of resources in reserve, and closer association always increased the esteem in which he was held.

He was exact but strictly honest in business affairs, charitable in his judgment of the motives and actions of others, modest and unassuming in manners, plain and economical in habits, and trusted by all whom he knew. His life was pervaded by an earnest, steadfast Christian purpose, and had it been spared to riper years, his continuing usefulness was assured, and his ultimate eminence in the honored profession he had chosen was highly probable. *"Requiescat in pace"* is the cordial wish of his classmate and chum.

Yours truly,   SAMUEL W. BUCK.

CHAPTER III.

I AM asked to say something of my intercourse with the late Joseph R. Davis, which was one of as warm regard and close intimacy as could exist between persons holding the relation first of teacher and pupil and again of principal and assistant in carrying on the Latin department in college. Davis entered college in 1872, and immediately gave token of becoming that most satisfactory of all persons to an instructor — a student who left no difficulty unsolved. I remember how, after a few weeks, when the freshmen had shaken themselves together, and their individual capacities had been made manifest to all, whenever a difficulty of translation or construction made it necessary to pause for inquiry and investigation, the eyes of every member of the class would turn for a solution of the puzzle to the quiet, steady-looking youth who sat apparently unmoved but always with a twinkle in his eye and the suspicion of a smile, and the knot must have been very complicated which he failed to disentangle.

With all this quiet sobriety of demeanor, he exhibited on occasion an unexpected faculty of humor. I will relate one little circumstance in which he was the chief actor, which will

(16)

illustrate my last assertion and will show in what way he affected others beside myself. At the end of the first term, when the class was assembled for examination, we were somewhat astonished to see a Dominie enter and announce that Dr. Potter had appointed him to examine the class. "All right ; sit down. Here is the book." He bade me call up some one. I thought it best to give him at once a dose that would satisfy him, so I called up Davis. We had the last three books of the Iliad to get through, and I put him to read the lament of Andromache at the tidings of Hector's death — a very pathetic and somewhat difficult passage. " Go on,". said I, and he began to read the passage in English in very good style. " Hold on," said the Dominie, " why does he not read the Greek ? " " That is not my way," I said. " However, Davis, read fifteen lines of Greek right off, and then return to your translation." He did so ; and having accomplished both satisfactorily, the model examiner began to ask him some baby questions in grammar, whereat I became impatient, and stopping him, said : " Davis, take that sentence and pull it to pieces and then put it together again." All which was done in such a manner that the Dominie rose, made him a bow, and troubled us no more then, or at any future examination. When our work was ended and the class dismissed Davis remained, and approaching me, said very quietly, with a cunning look : " Don't you think we settled the Dominie, Professor ? " I have just been looking over the record of his marks in my books, and I look almost with incredulity at the amazing string of 10's, an unbroken sequence of perfect marks in two studies, Latin and Greek, for a space of three full years. It seems wonderful that amid all the changes and chances of a student's career, with apparently no allowance for occasional weakness or wavering, there should have been through all that time no variableness or shadow of turning in the earnest striving after perfect accomplishment of the end in view. We can account for this if we bear in mind that he ever proved himself to be an essentially religious and conscientious person who had set before himself an exalted standard of duty to which he advanced always with an eye single and a step unswerving. Moreover, I imagine that he really had less difficulty in learning certain subjects than others have. His mental conformation was one calculated to enable him to cope with and overcome the perplexities of unknown tongues. I never had a pupil who showed equal analytical power in searching out and mastering the crudities of a complicated sentence. He may have obtained this facility by right of birth, for he belonged to the Welsh family of twisted tongues, to whom, as a compensation, nature has vouchsafed a remarkable power for the acquisition of language. Be the cause what it will, I repeat that he had great power in the mastering of Latin and Greek, and in imparting his knowledge to others.

Thus passed his years of early manhood, until he finished his college course and received all the honors we could bestow. Those of us who well knew him and his aims looked to the time when he would be welcomed into the educational force of the College as an undoubted certainty, for where could we look to find a man more fitted to help us by devotion to duty, by natural ability, by education and training to that particular end? He therefore became my assistant as tutor of Latin, with the expectation that in due course he would be promoted to the position of Professor of Latin. We looked forward with confident hope that at length Union College would have a professor in that department fully competent to its duties, regarded with respect and affection by all, both professors and undergraduates, as it has never been either before or since in my time. How this expectation was nullified I will leave others to say.

H. WHITEHORNE.

CHAPTER IV.

AS A STUDENT OF MATHEMATICS.

MR DAVIS' love for the pure mathematics, and the many useful and exquisitely beautiful applications which have been made of them to the physical sciences, gave sure promise that had he devoted his intellect to either pure or applied mathematics he would have achieved success in the chosen field of labor. His acquirements were such that during his college course he took the first rank as a student of those subjects. The work was in no sense mere lesson-getting, but it was in a large degree calculated to develop the power of original thought on the part of the student, and thus lead to true mental growth. The mere student of work done by others — the hard laborer on Calculus, Higher Mechanics, Quaternions, etc.— could not, during the past ten years, have taken high rank in Union College as a mathematician. To win that honor a man must possess real, native mathematical talent, and we believe that Mr. Davis was thus gifted. It is doubtful whether the marked ability shown by him in other branches is ever possessed by a student without the presence of the faculty to acquire high rank as a mathematician. Many students are placed under feeble-minded instructors for their early training, the faculty for mathematics is neglected, and it is then assumed that it does not exist. However, a close study of carefully arranged lists of great minds will, I believe, establish the proposition. At the celebration of the semi-centennial anniversary of the connection of Prof. Isaac W. Jackson with the faculty of Union College, Dr. Taylor Lewis spoke thus of the subject to which his friend, Dr. Jackson, had devoted his life : " Pure mathematics, so called from their crystal claritude, as compared with the mixed and physical branches. He has had a clear mind constantly gazing upon the *science of certainty;* a still higher title by which it may be called, in contrast with the dimness and doubt and shadow that rest upon almost all the provinces of human thought. Nor is it the less worth in respect to the dignity and elevation of its truth." Later, in his address on the same occasion, Dr. Lewis adds : " The pure geometry, as Plato would tell us, is inherent in the Divine mind, not made by God, as nature, but a part of His very being. It came forth at the command, ' Let there be light !' and stamped the dark outward world with its inward forms." Dr. Lewis devoted most of his life to the study of languages, but he never forgot the pleasure and strength which mathematical study had afforded him.

Mr. Davis looked forward eagerly, as he said to me, to the time when all the technical work of the Seminary should be completed and he should be settled in some church work. " Then, Professor, I can review my old mathematical studies and push on into new departments of the subject." He enjoy-ed, to the fullest measure, such work, and he saw and owned that he owed his finest discipline to mathematical studies.

CHAPTER V.

MR. DAVIS AS TUTOR OF LATIN IN UNION COLLEGE.

THE influence of scholarly students upon other students and upon the general character of the work done in a college cannot be over estimated. Mr. Davis entered the College at a time when some young professors and instructors were struggling hard against great odds to advance the course of study to such a degree that the bitterest enemy of the institution could no longer term it "Botany Bay." A strong party in the Faculty, and a majority of the Trustees, seemed to desire to give merely the value of a certificate of residence to the college diploma. The right prevailed, and by the aid of such students as Mr. Davis in giving a scholarly character to the work in the class rooms, and by their help afterwards as tutors, the scholarship of the institution was much advanced. Those who received diplomas between the years 1873–1883 may well feel proud of them. They represent a course in well-chosen branches of study, leading, in many cases, to rare scholarship, and in all to culture and refinement.

Mr. Davis was a member of the Faculty for three years. His work was in the Latin Department. At that time Professor Whitehorne, an Oxford scholar possessing rare gifts as a teacher and disciplinarian, was directing the work in the Department.   The Professor was Mr. Davis' former instructor and warm friend, and with the generous aid of the former Mr. Davis soon found that his Department was gaining a reputation for doing thorough work.   When Mr. Davis left the College he was rapidly taking a high position as an able teacher.   He loved teaching, but the advice of his dearest friends and his own longings to be doing the Master's work, were rapidly leading him towards the ministry.   From the day he entered Union Theological Seminary till he graduated, he felt that he had been guided by his Master's hand in choosing his life work ; and his teachers soon recognized his noble character and noted his remarkable scholarship.   While teaching in the College the students admired his unpretentious yet scholarly methods, and the Faculty were proud to name him as one of their body.   It is a law in Union College that the tutors must be elected yearly.   At the end of his third year Mr. Davis was not re-elected.   The circumstances attending the election of his successor were such that all men who loved Mr. Davis, and the simple honesty which marked every word and act of his short life, hasten to forget them.   The Faculty had lost a member of whose scholarship scholars speak with enthusiasm — one who favored high scholarship, and a relationship between college officers and pupils which should be marked by truthfulness and exalted moral purpose.

CHAPTER VI.

A LETTER FROM REV. DR. T. G. DARLING.

ALL through his college course and during his tutorship Mr. Davis was a zealous worker in the First Presbyterian Church, and its pastor, Rev. Dr. T. G. Darling has shown his warm appreciation of his work and character in the following letter :

FIRST PRESBYTERIAN CHURCH,
SCHENECTADY, N. Y., April 30, 1884.

My Dear Professor :— My inability to put on paper the feeling which I have as the result of my intercourse with our friend Mr. Davis, has caused my long delay in responding to your request for a sketch of his life in the church. Of the personal life, its sincerity and simplicity, you had the best possible opportunity to judge on the hill. The character which can for four years stand the test of college life, students and Faculty being judge, jury and witness, can stand any test — if there be a more searching one, it may, perhaps, be that of the instructor — where incompetency or untrustworthiness only need time to be detected and branded.

I shall speak, therefore, only of Mr. Davis' relation to our church and Christian work, and you can make as little or as much use of it as you please.

(24)

Mr. Davis united with this church October 25, 1877, coming to us from the First Congregational Church at Franklin, N. Y. I do not remember our first personal contact. I began to feel his help in the church before I really knew who he was, as you can readily understand might be with one so faithful and yet so unobtrusive, if not self-depreciating.

But from the time that his work pointed him out as one who did not belong to the great majority needing to be lifted, but to those who recognize their stewardship down to the day he left for the Seminary, I felt increasingly his force for good in the church, and leaned upon him with no fear of a fall.

His estimate of his own ability to render service was a very modest one, yet it never hindered him from assuming cheerfully, even if timidly, any duty which Providence seemed to lay at his door. If we were willing to assume the responsibility for possible failure, he was willing to assume the responsibility of doing the hard work, and it was not long before the duty became with him a prized privilege, for he loved the Lord's work and pulled always the laboring oar, not coveting an ornamental place in the stern.

In this way, in a relatively short time, he was identified with the best life and spiritual force of the church. All the workers knew and prized his coöperation, for he was always where he had promised to be, feeling that the lukewarmness or failure of others was an additional call to him to put in his best strength.

You know how accurate and painstaking and laborious he

was in all his college duties, in his eagerness to get as much and as varied knowledge as was possible, and to get it thoroughly, seeming always to be overtaxing his physical energies. It was, therefore, always a marvel to see how regularly he was in his place at the appointed meetings, and how scrupulously he attended to the details of committee work, especially in connection with the Young People's Association in which he held an honored position and influence, never suffering his religious work to be pushed aside by college or social engagements. He was a model of fidelity in every trust, and was soon, with possibly one exception, more closely and helpfully identified with all the interests of the church than any of the students who have so much helped the church during the past ten years. He was personally a great comfort to me in Christian work; for once he had become responsible for anything the whole burden of concern dropped from me, in the assured confidence that he would do his work with intelligent thoroughness and consecration. In all the time that he was with us — whether as student or instructor in college — I never knew him to seek to be excused from any work because it was difficult, or disagreeable, or discouraging. If he changed his work it was at our request to undertake something of more consequence, or which it was harder to find help than in the work which he was already prosecuting, and I do not recall his laying aside anything which he had not improved and advanced. He had a good Christian courage, for while he would state the reasons which, in his judgment, disqualified him from an undertaking—

and this with no mock modesty but from a serious distrust of his fitness — once it had been considered wise for him to put his hand to the plow he measured his work and put into it all his energies, apparently feeling that the less he was adapted to it the more force he would need to make good his lack of qualification. I need hardly say that he enjoyed the fullest confidence and esteem, and that he earned it.

He was very helpful in our prayer meetings, not often speaking, but with fervor and simplicity and great helpfulness taking frequent part in prayer. He was an intelligent and attractive and spiritually-minded teacher in the Sabbath School. One of his scholars, who happens to be with me as I write, says that the whole effort of his teaching was to bring the class to Christ, and that he seemed "alive with the Spirit." He followed up their conversion with efforts to make them feel their responsibility to engage in extra work, and it was through his efforts that the friend just referred to began public Christian work.

Knowing something of the time and strain involved in all this, you can judge that nothing but a most sincere devotion to Christ could ever have induced a man so busy and zealous in his studies to devote so much of his time and heart to religious work. If at the same time he was active in the religious life of the college — as I understand that his piety was as marked then as his scholarship — his endowments of grace and capacity for the maximum of work with the minimum of obtrusiveness were extraordinary ; for as I said it was the work always which pointed out the man, and not the man who was pointing out the work. He did "with his might" whatever his moral judgment directed him to do, and yet there was no indiscreet or fuming zeal about him, but intelligent conviction and progressive devotion to extra work as the main purpose of life. With all his love for study his life showed that back of the application, and deeper than the scholarly delight which he took in application, was the hope that all his acquisitions would prove a means to the end of building up Christ's kingdom.

It was not merely a personal and social grief to us when he left but a spiritual loss to the church, though we are grateful for the influence still living in us. When I visited his Seminary in New York the professors spoke in the highest terms of his character and scholarship, one of them saying: "Send us more men like Davis; he is the kind of man we need for the ministry."

In the summer vacation of '81 he took charge of the Park Place Chapel for us. He had previously found time in his busy life to make his influence felt there also, and was warmly welcomed back. The same characteristics which attended his former life and work among us were again exhibited. He was thorough rather than brilliant. He lacked the personal magnetism which attracts men suddenly, and unreasonably and independently of character. He planted deep, and was content to trust God for future results, more anxious about the root than the sudden sprouting. He was not the man to lose out of his hand what had already been acquired while grasping ambitiously after great things. Solid work, even if slow, was his aim, while he strove for permanence rather than popular impression.

After completing his Seminary course amid increasing infirmities, he came up for his examinations in Presbytery prior to ordination for missionary work in Southern California. He had, as was his habit, measured his work carefully, knew just what was expected of him, and without any seeming consciousness that he was distinguishing himself passed, wherever he was tested, a most complete and satisfactory examination, showing himself, as we all expected, entirely at home in all the subjects in which the examination was not merely formal.

As I look back on his life among us and think of his mingled strength and simplicity, his loyalty to truth, his sincere devotion, his unaffected unconsciousness of his own merit, his work so unobtrusive that we measured it by its helpfulness rather than the conspicuousness of the agent, the uncomplaining cheerfulness with which, in the midst of the pressure of his college duties, he let us put on him the hard work to which some other could not be kept steady, not relinquishing anything till it was accomplished. I feel how strange was the human or "wrong" side of the Providence who, at the threshold of its earthly ministry, took away the life so hard to replace to fill the grave so much more easily filled. It is hard to think of all the stored knowledge and accumulated energy and consecration of his life which he could not leave to another being lost to a world which so much needed it. It must be that all the sympathy which quickened his labors, and the discipline which ripened his spirit, and the acquired gifts which made his labor so efficient and filled us all with such hope for his future have been transferred of God to a broader field, and the talents which faithfulness doubléd made the working capital for more extended usefulness in the larger things over which the Master has made him ruler.

Yours faithfully,

T. G. Darling.

CHAPTER VII.

KANSAS CITY, June 23, 1883.

WE were hindered by the rain, so that we did not reach here until about daybreak to-day, whereas we should have reached here last evening; and it is raining hard here this morning. It is quite unlikely that I shall see my brother to-day because of a washout in the road leading thither. The agent tells me now that he thinks I can go, but will be able to tell me more definitely when the time comes for the train to go, 8.50. I hope I shall get there, but am not very confident.

I passed the time as pleasantly as I could at Eldon and also at Trenton, another station where we stopped two or three hours yesterday afternoon. I was feeling pretty well aside from the aggravation of being delayed. The weather was pleasant where we had to wait, although we had two or three showers when we were travelling. I expected when I left home to reach Chicago Wednesday night, this place the night following, and have all day Friday to go to my brother's, but you see how the rains just spoiled all my plans. I would not mind it very much if I could get to Carson to-day.

(31)

We nearly ate the people at Eldon out of everything they
had, for the place is not very large, and there was a large
number of us ; there was a dining car on the train out from
Chicago, and that was left for us to feed the hungry and
impatient crowd.   Indeed you may believe it was just charm-
ing, staying there where there was nothing to be seen and
nothing much to do but wait for the time to go by !   The
river was so high the cars had to stop, I should think, three or
four miles away, and we were brought over in a miserable old
river steamboat.   We had a dreary thunder shower as we
were about to leave the cars which kept us in them until the
rain was over.   *   *   *   I am still feeling well, but at
present a little tired.   I hope to get refreshed and ready for
a new start at Carson.

Just before leaving his brother's he writes, June 30, concerning the work in which he is about to engage :

I am anxious to get there (Riverside) for I fear the people
will be impatient at my delay.   (They were expecting him
early in June.)   I am more anxious still about the work that
is to follow, and with what satisfaction and success I shall per-
form it !   I have done nothing scarcely in the way of preparation for it, except to refrain almost entirely from all mental
labor, and I fear it will take me some time to get into the
harness.   However, I shall try to avoid borrowing trouble and
endeavor to trust in the Lord ; if it be His will that I labor
successfully at Riverside, He will be with me, and if it is not,
then the sooner I find it out the better.   I almost tremble

when I think of the responsibility, and yet I believe it has not been my own seeking.

RIVERSIDE, July 9, 1883.

You do not know how glad I am to get to my journey's end. I was getting weary and anxious to get among civilized people. I am afraid it would try me more than I thought to labor on the frontier among all classes of people, particularly among those who have no reverence for the Bible or for God's house.   '

Thus far I am more than delighted with the place ; it seems queer to me, however, that there is no fear of rain or of cloudy weather until November or December. The sky is bright and clear. This valley is fresh and green, in marked contrast with the sandy plain and naked mountains about here.

I think I am improving in health.

RIVERSIDE, Aug. 3, 1883.

Long before this reaches you the work which is now staring me in the face will be ended in some way or other. Next Sabbath we have communion, and to-morrow afternoon at three o'clock a preparatory service was to be held ; that would keep me pretty busy, though I could see my way clear all right. This morning, however, I was waited upon by a young man who informed me of the death of his cousin, who had been sick for over three weeks. He died last night; service is to be at the house to-morrow at 3 P. M., and I am asked to conduct the service. So there is additional labor. The preparatory lecture will have to be appointed for Saturday evening,

I presume, though I am not sure what arrangement has been made. I am a little afraid of my strength.

Saturday, 5.20 P. M.— I have just returned from the funeral service and the elders very kindly have omitted the preparatory service, so that I am at liberty until to-morrow. I got through the exercises this afternoon full as well as I expected. There was a male quartette to do the singing, and I read portions of Scripture, offered prayer and made a few remarks from Ps. 102, 24.

Next week Mr. C. and I are thinking of going to the coast for a week or so. The session are willing to give me a rest of a couple of weeks, and we are thinking of trying the effect of sea air upon me. The place to which we are going is called Willmore City.

WILLMORE CITY, Aug. 9, 1883.

As you see, I am at the sea coast, and the Pacific is grand as the great waves come rolling into the shore hour after hour. There are perhaps half a dozen buildings here which are called houses. They are boarded up and down with red wood, the cracks battened and the inside papered, but not plastered. There is one building sided and painted white, owned by parties from Riverside, which looks quite like a house, and another in process of erection which will be very comfortable when completed. There are fifteen or twenty tents along the edge of the bluff and a temporary bath house. This is Willmore City—very preposessing, do you not think so?

I am writing in our room in what is called by way of compliment and by a great extension of the term, a hotel, the only one here. I can see the ocean from my window and watch the waves as they break upon the shore.

We started Tuesday at 6 A. M. and reached here at 6 P. M., or a little later. The ride was as pleasant as any ride of fifty miles across the country can be here. The road in some places was so sandy that we could not drive off of a walk, and the horses sank in almost up to their ankles. We stopped at noon by the roadside in the shade of some cottonwood trees and fed our horses and ate our dinner. The chief drawback was the want of good water to drink. We were near two houses but they had no well and used water drawn from the irrigating ditch. We set out again in an hour and rode through two miles or more of white river sand and then came to a town called Anaheim.

Then we rode across a plain with no habitation for six or eight miles certainly, until we came to a large house on a rise of ground. We rode nearly six miles further over a very interesting road, and finally reached Willmore City. How my bright anticipations vanished when I saw the place! I expected to find a small village with streets regularly laid out and a hotel of some pretentions, but I had no right to any such anticipation, for though the place is advertised quite extensively, and maps are published giving the names of the streets and various other things which are misleading, the place is only a year or less in age—it is mushroom growth. Supplies of provisions are brought from Wilmington, three or

four miles away, to which one can go in part by street car, in
part by steam car.

Thursday, 3 P. M.—I took a walk after dinner, but the
wind is a great deal cooler to-day than yesterday. I felt it
quite cool when I went down to the beach; in fact it was too
cool to be comfortable. * * * So far as comfort and en-
joyment are concerned, I had much rather be in R.; but if it
will be good for me here, why this is the place for me, I
fancy.

RIVERSIDE, Aug. 19, 1883.

(After his return from the coast.)

The next day after our return I thought myself a great deal
better than when I went away; but the day following I did
not feel nearly so well, and all the week I have felt rather
miserable. I do not know what it means; my appetite is not
so good, and if that fails I do not know what will happen. I
felt pretty well at the coast until the day we left—then I was
not so vigorous. On the whole, I did not like Willmore City
any too well; it was pretty cool for me at times, and I was
not so comfortable for that reason. I spent a good part of
the time out of doors, but it was fearfully monotonous
for me.

I went to see the doctor this morning; he does not seem
to think that I am any worse; advised me to try the mountain air, and I am thinking seriously of going on Monday to
Crafton, 28 miles from here, to stay until next Saturday, at
least. I do not gain in strength, but Crafton may help me.

CRAFTON, Aug. 22, 1883.

I came to this place last Monday; one of our elders brought me up and returned the next day—yesterday. He came purposely to bring me a distance of twenty miles or more off toward the mountains; if the people are not kind to me, then I am mistaken.

My going to the coast, on the whole, I guess, was no gain to me—whatever it might have proved had I not gone into the ocean. As a matter of fact, I am no better, and my going into the water was probably a mistake. My appetite is not so good as it was before I began wandering around.

, I like the surroundings here very much; there is grass about the house and plenty of shade, a walk by the side of the brook, and seats here and there, so that in these respects it is very pleasant. Thursday morning, I do not know whether I am any better here than at R. or not; have not been here long enough yet, and then, too, I was very tired when I arrived here on Monday. We had been nearly eight hours on the road, and though while we were riding I was not conscious of being weary; after we reached here I felt more completely worn out than I have yet felt on this coast. I am ashamed of myself to think that I can endure so little.

Yesterday I spent most of the time in reading the " Inde- pendent," " Memorials of a Quiet Life," and some, though not as much as I ought, in the Bible. To-day the Bible and Wordsworth have occupied me thus far.

It does not require much exertion to use me up, and I feel somehow that I must do something if I am to receive the

greatest possible benefit.   The sun is so hot that I have an
aversion to being out in it, and so I loaf, and read, and walk a
little ; this morning I took a horseback ride of a couple of
miles or so.   I do not know whether I am going to get very
strong in one week more ; I believe I am feeling better.   I
trust that by-and-by improvement will be more rapid.

CRAFTON, Aug. 29, 1883.

It is warm here, even if it is a little elevated, shaded and
furnished with water in a running stream.   It is sometimes
quite uncomfortable because of the sultryness combined with
the heat.

Yesterday and to-day have witnessed a little horseback riding ; I rode six miles to-day, and did it without much fatigue.
I still have a cough and some pain in my side, but I think I
am improving ; people tell me that I look better, and so I
suppose I really am better, but my strength is not much and
my breath would soon be goone if I undertook any severe
exertion.

I am going to stay here one week longer at any rate, and
indeed in my present condition I do not feel that I can carry
the work required of me during a year unless help comes
from somewhere.

Friday morning.—I believe I can still give an encouraging
report of myself.   I am sure I am better than when I came to
California, and think I have improved ever since coming here.
But one has to be so careful against taking cold, because of the
great difference in temperature between night and day.   At

night sometimes the mercury stands at 54°, and during the day it may be from 95° to 100° or more—a very great change in twenty-four hours.

This is quite an out of the way place, although we get mail every day. There are only four or five houses beside this one in this immediate vicinity, and that completes Crafton ; then the road passes through a dry plain with no houses for a distance ; further on (3 miles from here) is Lugonia, where we get our mail. The same building is a store, postoffice and dwelling house ; there are four or five houses beside, and that is all of Lugonia. The country around is barren, principally ; on some, peaches, oranges, apples and grapes are raised, the soil being irrigated by water from the stream which runs past here.

CRAFTON, Sept. 4, 1883.

I am feeling pretty well to-day, and in the morning of every day can get along very well, but the middle of the day is *so* hot. I have finished the first volume of "Memorials of a Quiet Life," and have enjoyed it so much. What beautiful dispositions Mr. and Mrs. Augustus Hare had—so thankful to God for His gifts, and so dilligent in serving Him by working in various ways for men.

We have not had a good wetting rain since I have been here, and are not likely to have for some time to come. Fruit growers do not want to see rain until all their grapes are dried, as moisture spoils them.

Return to Riverside to-morrow.

RIVERSIDE, Sept. 10, 1883.

As you see, I am back home again—came Wednesday, as expected. I did not preach yesterday, though I fully intended to do so when I came home. But my shortness of breath under any continued exertion is so great that I did not think it wise to venture. Unfortunately, I took a little cold while at Crafton, and added to it quite a good deal the next day after coming home.

We had a meeting of the session yesterday and they granted me a release for September and October, I to furnish suitable supply during that time. Mr. Condit may leave some time in October, and whenever he leaves I shall have to assume the work, for I do not know of any one else to obtain. I greatly hope that I may improve rapidly in a short time, and as we are now approaching the winter season, which is said to be the best, perhaps I may get along very well. God grant that I may, for I know not what to do if such should not be the result.

RIVERSIDE, Sept. 14, 1883.

I purchased a horse last Monday and since that time I have been riding out a little morning and afternoon. I go soon after breakfast, and usually get back about 11 o'clock. Then I rest awhile and read something until dinner; after dinner I read again for a time or write until about 4 o'clock, when I go out and stay until six. I hope for great benefit from horseback riding.

Next week Tuesday the Los Angeles Presbytery, in which

we are, meets at Los Angeles. I suppose I shall be there
and shall have an opportunity of seeing a place about which
I have heard so much.

Did you know that we have slight earthquake shocks here
occasionally? We have had only one since I have been here
that I have felt, and I was then at Crafton. There was only
one shock there, but here in R. they say there were three. It
was past before I realized what it was; it was a sort of rumbling
and jarring combined. I do not know exactly how to
describe it: one could feel a slight movement of some kind,
but it was gone in a moment. People here feel very secure
when they read of the cyclones and dreadful storms in the
east; they think themselves free from anything of that kind,
and indeed I suppose they are.

RIVERSIDE, Sept. 22, 1883.

I attended the meeting of the Presbytery at Los Angeles;
was there two days and was present at all the sessions. We
went by rail from Colton; I do not know the distance. Mr.
C., who was the delegate from Arlington, and myself had as
pleasant a ride as one can have in riding over a country like
this, where there is little or no vegetation and no dwelling
houses save in the towns.

I am now a member of Los Angeles Presbytery, and no
longer of Albany. I did not see much of the city, but think
it a rather pleasant place; it was not so hot as it has been
here—yesterday 110°, and to-day the same. That is not
a California story but an actual fact! The city is built in a

valley and on high bluffs, very steep, and from the bluffs one gets a fine view, but he earns it in climbing.

How the time goes by ! I just realize to-day that there is only one week more of this month. Soon October will be over, and then I must go to work. I am bound to be much stronger by that time or I fear I shall make a poor showing. I am not fit to preach ; I *ought* to be preaching now, and I do not know how soon I shall be able to preach again.

NORDHOFF, CAL., Oct. 5, 1883.

This place is distant thirty-seven miles from Santa Barbara and fifteen miles from San Buena Ventura on the coast, in what is called the Ojai valley, almost completely shut in by mountains.

I went by stage from R. to Colton, a week ago last Monday afternoon, in order to take the early train to Los Angeles the next morning. I went on the next morning and stayed in Los Angeles until afternoon when the train ran to San Pedro, where I was to take the steamer to Santa Barbara. Arrived in Santa Barbara Wednesday afternoon, and was told that there was no daily stage to the Ojai, as I had previously been informed. There was only a stage on Tuesday of each week. Santa Barbara was no place for me, I knew, because of the dampness, and I was bound to go away from there as soon as I could. I inquired about the different ways of reaching here, and the earliest that I learned was to take a steamer Friday night back to San Buena Ventura. I concluded I would go Thursday morning by stage to San Marcus

Grade back of Santa Barbara up in the mountains to a place recommended me, and if I found it good I would stay there.

What a climb we had. It was quite exciting to *me*, and would have been much more interesting were it not for that fact. We went up a steep grade, for I know not how many miles, up, up, up, with very sharp turns every now and then, a high bank of rock, perhaps, on one side and a precipice on the other. Large rocks were coming to the surface and formed the bed of the road in many places. In one place the road was cut through the solid rock, and was so steep that furrows had been cut in the rock so that the horses might cling to it. I was a little alarmed when we were going over that, and was very thankful when it was passed. But the view was magnificent! You could look down on the lower ridges and ravines as they wound in and out among each other, see the valleys far away and the rocks and trees all around you. They were not very large trees, chiefly live-oak — a very hardy sort of scrubby wood which grew so thickly as to cover everything up — and you saw green leaves all around. Before we were *near* the top I could feel that the air was rarer, though I could breathe without any great difficulty. We reached the summit and began to descend before we came to a single habitation, and the first we came to was my destination. The place recommended to me was reached. Not very inviting I said to myself for a stay of any length. A house one-story, boarded up and down with rough boards covered with whitewash (an item in its favor), a barren door-yard with a sluggish stream in front from which bad odors proceeded. The lady was kind but could not accommodate me, and especially that day, for a friend was coming to visit her and would arrive in a short time with the stage from the opposite direction. Didn't I feel discouraged ! here I had taken that long ride, longer than I had taken before since coming from Crafton, and I was a little apprehensive about the effect of the ride back the same day without resting, but I stood it better than I anticipated, and after the night's rest felt quite refreshed. We went down the mountain pretty rapidly, and did not have so much chance to admire the scenery as when we went up. There were four horses, and about all they did was to guide the stage and keep out of its way. The driver puts his foot on the brake — a large heavy one that would keep the wheels from turning sometimes — and away we went. There was one place, however, over that bare rock where he made the horses walk very slowly, but in other places it was quite different. Next morning I took the stage from Santa Barbara for Ventura — a stage which, I learned, ran every day, though the hotel proprietors did not tell me of it. I had good fare — excellent — at the " Arlington," but I cannot quite forgive them for keeping me in ignorance of that stage.

I think I am some better here, and yet I do not know. Yesterday was cloudy and quite cold. I was cold about noon, and sat for some time after dinner in front of the parlor fire trying to get warm. To-day is clear and warm, and I feel better, but there is a good deal of difficulty in breathing, more than I have felt before. I do not know what it means — whether it is something temporary or in the natural course of the disease. I cough a good deal at night, but less, I think, than when I came. I suppose there is some wise purpose in it all, but sometimes I feel a little *discouraged*.

NORDHOFF, Oct. 12, 1883.

Yes, my alloted time of rest is rapidly passing, and yet I do not think the people will ask me to do what they think I cannot without injury to myself. I do not know what will be the outcome, but I fear I shall not be strong enough to do good work Nov. 1st. I am thinking of going back to R. next Wednesday, whatever I do afterwards.

RIVERSIDE, Oct. 19, 1883.

You will see by this that I am back in my old quarters, reaching here yesterday, as I expected, and was glad to be at my journey's end; was some tired, but not seriously. It seems natural and good to be back again, but whether it will be as beneficial remains to be seen.

I had written thus far, when it occurred to me it was time to see whether my pony had forgotten how to carry me or not. He has grown a little frisky in my absence, but he went all right; there was nothing to be noted about him, except that he seemed to have lost familiarity with objects along the road, and had the whole thing to learn over again. I had a dreadful stage ride in getting to the depot, at Newhall, on Wednesday. The roads were very dusty, as only California roads can be, and the stage was drawn by four horses. Perhaps you can imagine what a dust they would kick up, and then the stage must pass through that raised dust and the passengers must breathe it. Sometimes there would be a breeze across our path or in our faces, and oh, how refreshing — for it carried the dust away, and we could get a little *pure* air. Besides this, there was the roughness of the roads. In this country there are a great many very heavy loads drawn of grain, wood, or something else, and they cut up the roads badly. They use four, six, and sometimes even more horses. Then there are holes in the road, round or oblong, just large enough to let the wheel down; they are called chuck holes, and correctly, for the way the stage chucks into them makes me wish the journey over. The distance was thirty-seven miles, and I was glad, indeed, to stop. I had ridden already that day before taking the stage thirteen miles in a private convey-ance, and it made a pretty hard day of it. I went from Nordhoff to Santa Paula, and then took the stage to Newhall. In the morning I took the train to Colton and the stage to R., reaching here about noon.

———

Thus the story of his experiences in California ends. In a few weeks after the date of this last letter he reached home. Of the details of the homeward journey we are ignorant.

CHAPTER VIII.

A LETTER FROM REV. DR. GEORGE ALEXANDER.

DR. ALEXANDER knew Mr. Davis as a co-laborer in the Union College Faculty, and the following letter attests that he warmly appreciated his virtues :

UNIVERSITY PLACE CHURCH, }
NEW YORK, Feb. 22, 1884. }

My Dear Prof. Price :—You ask me to contribute something to your contemplated Memoir of our friend J. R. Davis. I am glad to know that there is to be some recognition of his worth besides the silent memorial of mound and stone, but I regret that I have so little to say concerning one who deserves so much. I had not the advantage of knowing him as a student, and during our brief association in the College Faculty I was so cumbered with many things that I had but little time to penetrate the mantle of his reserve and find the man. Now that he has passed from us to goodlier fellowship, I realize that it is a mistake not to find time for the cultivation of such a friendship. I do not find it easy to describe the prominent features of his character. He was devoid of those eccentricities which often secure attention and reputation for inferior merit. There was nothing exaggerated or one-sided about him. Both in mind and character he was symetrical,

(47)

well-poised, and this gave a quiet dignity to his speech and bearing. I admired his scholarship, unalloyed as it was by any conceit of attainment ; I coveted his power of brief, terse statement ; but most of all I was impressed by his clear convictions, deep rooted principles, transparent honesty. I never suspected him of an ulterior motive or a suppressed purpose. In his chosen profession, where intellectual brilliancy counts for so little, where moral and spiritual soundness count for so much, I had anticipated for him a career of great usefulness and success. The disappointment of this hope confirms the larger hope of a life to come, in which the broken promise of the present may find fulfilment.

Sincerely yours,

GEORCE ALEXANDER.

CHAPTER IX.

THE Rev. Dr. Hastings, of Union Theological Seminary, furnished, through the Rev. Dr. Darling, the following very just tribute to Mr. Davis's character and scholarship. He says:

"There is but one feeling in the Faculty with regard to Mr. Davis's character and scholarship — he was respected and beloved by all his teachers. During his senior year I saw him personally (for private criticism) a good deal, as I do all of the seniors. I was deeply impressed with the solidity and strength of his nature; with the simplicity, sincerity and consecration of his Christian character. There was a poise, a steadiness, in his quiet energy which commanded respect from all. His scholarship was remarkable, but with it there were none of the usual signs of vanity or of self-consciousness. Noticing his failing health, I persuaded him to let me arrange for him an interview with the specialist, Dr. Loomis; and on Dr. Loomis' advice I secured Mr. Davis an appointment to go to Southern California. Mr. Davis advised with me frequently about this matter, and I was struck by the calmness with which he contemplated the critical con-

(49)

dition of his health; it was very unusual. The climate of Southern California did not help him, and he longed for home. I shall not soon forget his letters on this subject—so pathetic and so Christian were they in their deep resignation.

I think it should be said that Mr. Davis, without in the least seeking it, won not only the thorough respect, but the *affection* of his classmates to an unusual degree. We can see now how his character was ripening for Heaven, though we thought it was for distinguished usefulness on earth.

Yours very truly,   T. S. HASTINGS.

CHAPTER X.

ALTHOUGH Mr. Davis died on the 15th of January, it was not till late in February that the sad news reached his friends at Union ; and at the first meeting of the College Faculty, held after the reception of the news, the following resolution was unanimously adopted :

Resolved, That we learn with great regret of the recent death of our friend aud former colleague, the Rev. Joseph R. Davis.

As a student, we always found him industrious and successful, true to all his duties, honorable towards all men, and loyal to his Christian professions. As a teacher, these noble traits grew in intensity and earnestness, and became the brightest ornaments of a manly character. His humility of bearing and unassuming nature were alike attractive to his pupils and fellow teachers. We loved him for his generous worth ; we prized him for his talents, and saw in him possibilities of a future alike useful to humanity and his church. While we deeply mourn his loss, we tenderly sympathize with those to whom he was bound by the strong ties of family affection and love.

CHAPTER XI.

gT was the custom of Mr. Davis to spend a part of each long vacation, during his college course, at Neath, Pa., where his father resided. He was not averse to laboring on the farm during those periods; and he often talked to me of the great pleasure he felt at being in the hay field—renewing the experiences of his happy youth.

The Rev. Mr. Morris, pastor of the church at Neath, contributed the following very interesting account of Mr. Davis's connection with his church and his work; and, in addition, he gives many interesting details of his young friend's life:

NEATH, PA., May 2, 1884.

Prof. I. B. Price, Union College, N. Y.

DEAR SIR.—I am very glad that you have undertaken to prepare a memoir of the Rev. J. R. Davis; for a memoir of him is certainly very much to be desired, and it is especially fitting that it should come from Union College. When I became pastor of the church at Neath, in 1871, Mr. Davis had been a member of the church for a number of years; and, though quite young, he was already a marked man, and the church, together with the venerable pastor, the Rev. S. A.

(52)

Williams, had signified to him their strong conviction that he ought to devote himself to the Christian ministry. It was a long time after that before he saw his way clear to enter the ministry as a profession; but he had entered upon *the work* of the ministry almost from the beginning of his Christian life. At least, throughout the period of my acquaintance with him he was not only a devout and earnest believer, but also a zealous Evangelist and a thoughtful and devoted shepherd of the flock of Christ. He did nothing through strife or vain glory; he believed firmly and fervently, and therefore did he speak. He labored for souls because the love of Christ constrained him. He was always interested and helpful in the public services of the church; and, in the wider field of secular life, he attached himself in true human fellowship to all sorts and conditions of men. He let his light shine wherever he went; but he never forgot for a moment that he was not the light, but was sent to bear witness of the light. When he left home for college, I had the most absolute confidence that he would come out a still stronger and better man; but I wondered what temporary effect the distraction of many studies, and of new scenes and mixed society, might have on his religious spirit and habits. As he came among us from time to time during his vacations, I soon found that there was not to be even a momentary wavering. His attendance at all church services was as steady as ever, and his prayers and exhortations were more and more earnest and thoughtful. He visited the sick and the aged throughout the neighborhood. He watched the progress and declensions of his young friends so closely that, though he was away from home so much, I, who was on the ground all the time, had my attention first called to important matters by him quite frequently. I never knew any one more thoroughly possessed by the true pastoral spirit than he was; and I never knew any one who more ardently desired, or more faithfully prepared himself, to do a great work for Christ in the world. " Thou didst well in that it was in thine heart." The will was accepted for the work on earth, and he is transferred to the higher ministry of Heaven.

I am, dear sir, yours very truly,　　　　E. I. MORRIS.

CHAPTER XII.

THE END.

*g*T was on the 15th of May, 1883, that he preached his trial
sermon before the Albany Presbytery, which was in
session at Schenectady. At the same meeting he was
examined by a committee of the Presbytery. Everything
being satisfactory he stood fully equipped for doing Christ's
work, and talked anxiously of the time when he should be
at his post at Riverside, Southern California. This place
had been selected and secured for him by Dr. Hastings
of the Seminary. Only a little while had elapsed between the
Seminary examinations and those imposed by the Presbytery.
At the conclusion of the latter, though it was a better measure
of what the examiners had forgotten than of what the candidate
knew, he was much exhausted ; and to those who knew him
well he appeared too much broken down to undertake anything
but the rebuilding of his shattered health. As he entered
upon the long journey to California, which was to be broken
by only a few short stops for rest, it appeared plain to many
that, instead of hastening on to begin life's work, he was
nearing the great shadow which all too soon would fall full
across his path, and darken into the night when no man

(55)

can work. You have read the Memoir and know how it all ended. He died at his home, in Neath, on the 15th of January, 1884.

Bacon regarded as the gift of death, that "it openeth the gate to good fame and extinguisheth envy"; but our departed friend sought no fame which could be the gift of either life or death, and envy had no sting for him as he trod the narrow way and passed within the veil.